I0067163

Two Nickels Holding Up a Dollar

Dr. Angela Banner Joseph

Illustrated by:

Abira Das

i

Cover and text layout by Stanley Joseph Leslie

Copyright © 2015 by Dr. Angela Banner Joseph. All rights reserved.
No part of this book may be produced or utilized in any form or
by any means, electronic or mechanical, including photocopying, recording,
or by any information storage or retrieval system, without permission in writing
from the author. Inquiries should be addressed to
Dr.AngelaJoseph@gmail.com

Manufactured in the United States of America

For Samiya, Vida, and Ellie Rose

Foreword

This book is dedicated to all children who want to learn about money and saving. It is about learning the value of a dollar and sharing with you the importance of how to manage the most important commodity in the world: your own money.

You might have heard your parents, teachers, and friends talk about how money is important in your daily living. Did you know that money is an essential trading tool in the world? You can use money to pay your bills, purchase a car, pay your college tuition, buy a house, or just about anything you want to do. It is very important for you to learn to save your money.

In this book, I provide you with great advice, using words from people of all ages and occupations, about this thing called "money + saving." I wanted to write a book that would capture your heart and mind as you thought about money and the importance of saving for your future. This book is dedicated to you, and I want you to believe it was written especially for you.

I hope you will ask questions after you have read this book. Please talk to your parents, grandparents, aunts, uncles, teachers, friends, and mentors about what you learn from this book. Thank you for giving me an opportunity to open your mind about the topic of money.

"Rule No. 1: Never lose money. Rule No. 2: Never forget rule No. 1."

— *Warren Buffet*

"Everyone wants to ride with you in the limo, but what you want is someone who will take the bus with you when the limo breaks down."

— *Oprah Winfrey*

"Too many people spend money they earned...to buy things they don't want...to impress people that they don't like."

— Will Rogers

"Money... is like a beautiful thorough-bred horse--very powerful & always in action, but unless this horse is trained when very young, it will be an out-of-control & dangerous animal when it grows to maturity."

— Dave Ramsey

"I have too many credit cards. You know what happened? Someone stole one and I didn't notice. I noticed when I got that bill. Whoa! It was so much less! I'm letting him keep it. I'm saving money!"

— *Rita Rudner*

"When I was young I thought that money was the most important thing in life; now that I am old I know that it is."

— Oscar Wilde

"Don't spend your life working for money; save money and hire it to work for you."

— Dr. John F Demartini

"The safest way to double your money is to fold it over and put it in your pocket."

— *Kin Hubbard*

"If you think nobody cares if you're alive, try missing a couple of car payments."

— *Earl Wilson*

"It is never too early to encourage long-term savings."

— Ron Lewis

"Bills travel through the mail at twice the speed of checks."

— Steven Wright

"I can't picture in my mind three hundred and sixty thousand dollars... When I think of it, all I can see in my mind is a big nickel."

— *Harlan Ellison*

"I'll flick a penny to the dirt, and if I see one on the ground I won't pick it up. So why is .99 cents so much better than a dollar?"

— *Jarod Kintz*

"Saving entails sacrifice; maybe that's why it brings rewards. Those that save always have. If tomorrow you face a problem -you lose your job or your business, you know you can survive until the situation improves or you start another business, this time with firm foundations. However those that do not save..."

— *Mauricio Chaves Mesén*

"When you have money, think of the time when you had none."

— Japanese Proverb

"If a man empties his purse into his head, no one can take it away from him. An investment in knowledge always pays the best interest."

— *Benjamin Franklin*

"Find your own style. Don't spend your savings trying to be someone else. You're not more important, smarter, or prettier because you wear a designer dress."

— Salma Hayek

"One penny may seem to you a very insignificant thing, but it is the small seed from which fortunes spring."

— Orison Swett Marden

"Never spend your money before you have it."

— *Thomas Jefferson*

"Never stand begging for that which you have the power to earn."

— Miguel de Cervantes

"When I earn my first money, I went to a shop and bought jeans and a top. But then I wore them both for such a long time that finally my model agency said, 'You should buy something else!' I was saving the money because it was the first time I'd ever had any."

— *Olga Kurylenko*

"Make the most of online banking to make your life easier and keep your finances organized. Online banking is great because it offers quick, easy, 24-hour access to your checking and savings accounts."

— *Alexa Von Tobel*

"What we really want to do is what we are really meant to do. When we do what we are meant to do, money comes to us, doors open for us, we feel useful, and the work we do feels like play to us."

— *Julia Cameron*

"You can only become truly accomplished at something you love. Don't make money your goal. Instead, pursue the things you love doing, and then do them so well that people can't take their eyes off you."

— *Maya Angelou*

"You must gain control over your money or the lack of it will forever control you."

— Dave Ramsey

Dr. Angela Banner Joseph was born in Belize, Central America and has been employed at the City University of New York School of Law since 1991 as Director of Financial Aid. She earned her doctorate from the School of Educational Leadership for Change at the Fielding Graduate University, Santa Barbara, California. Dr. Joseph received a Master of Arts degree in Urban Affairs from Queens College of the City University of New York and a Bachelor's Degree in Sociology from the State University of New York at Stony Brook. She lives in New York City.

Thank you for purchasing this book. I am grateful. You can reach me at Dr.AngelaJoseph@gmail.com or www.Drangelabannerjoseph.com

www.ingramcontent.com/pod-product-compliance
Lightning Source LLC
Chambersburg PA
CBHW052053190326
41519CB00002BA/213